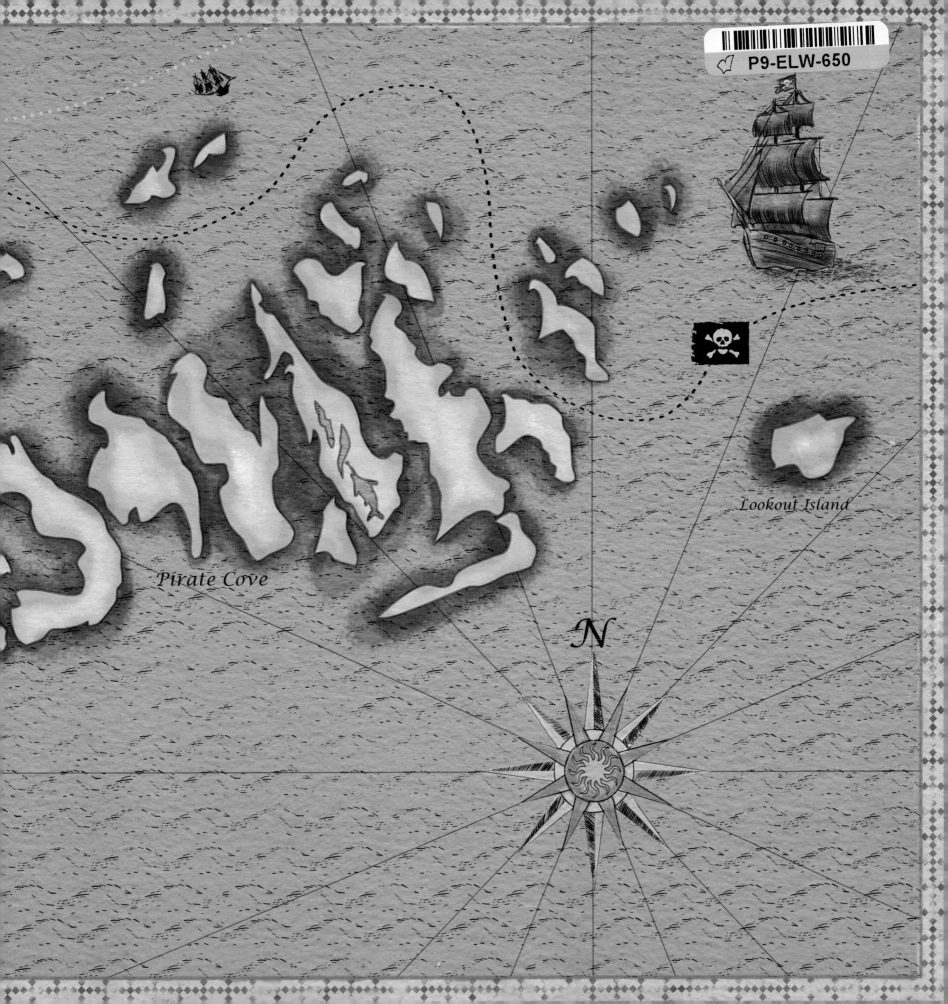

Pirate Cove

Lookout Island

N

Can You See What I See?
Treasure Ship

by Walter Wick

SCHOLASTIC INC.

New York   Toronto   London   Auckland
Sydney   Mexico City   New Delhi   Hong Kong

Can you see

what I see?

A whale's tail,

3 birds in the air,

a broken heart,

long flowing hair,

a lightning bolt,

an anchor, 3 keys,

a sun, a moon,

7 palm trees,

a shell from the sea,

a snake coiled up,

a spyglass, and

a golden cup!

Can you see
what I see?
A sea creature
with 8 long arms,
a gold bracelet
with 5 gold charms,
a unicorn,
a feather, a frog,
a cat with spots,
a dragon, a dog,
a scary skull face,
a golden door,
a diamond saber,
and much, much more!

Can you see
what I see?
3 butterflies,
a dragonfly, too,
a pig, 4 turtles,
2 hearts of blue,
a peacock, a carriage,
scissors, a spoon,
a bee in a box,
a sun near a moon,
2 gold sea horses,
a lizard, 5 fish,
an old cannonball,
and a broken dish!

Can you see
what I see?
A horse, 3 camels,
a lion, a lamb,
an owl, a snake,
a rooster, a ram,
a swan that's silver,
a key that's brass,
a pocket watch,
and an hourglass,
a cannon, a shark,
a curious eel,
a spider crab,
and a ship's wheel!

Can you see
what I see?
A heart of gold,
a diamond ring,
a sword for a knight,
a crown for a king,
an octopus,
a pearl in a shell,
a hammerhead shark,
4 turtles, a bell,
an elephant teapot,
a clothespin clip,
the tattered sails
of an old wrecked ship!

The Wreck of the *Bountiful*

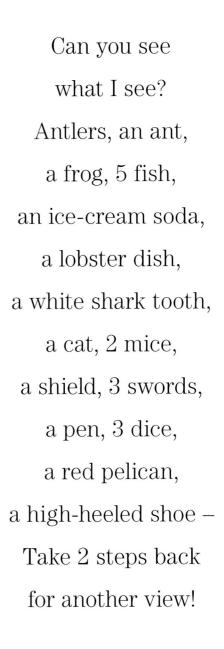

Can you see
what I see?
Antlers, an ant,
a frog, 5 fish,
an ice-cream soda,
a lobster dish,
a white shark tooth,
a cat, 2 mice,
a shield, 3 swords,
a pen, 3 dice,
a red pelican,
a high-heeled shoe –
Take 2 steps back
for another view!

Can you see
what I see?
A penguin, a pail,
a climbing man,
3 whales, a walrus,
a watering can,
an alligator,
a silver spring,
a mug, 2 monkeys,
an eyeball ring,
a bell, a bugle,
and bottles galore –
You're not done yet;
there's more to explore!

Can you see
what I see?
A fishing pole,
a goose that's green,
3 ship wheels,
a submarine,
a crab on a plate,
a rubber band,
a treasure chest
that's in the sand,
a surfboard for
a wild wave ride –
The weather's fine;
let's go outside!

Can you see
what I see?
A ship propeller,
a hammer, 2 saws,
an arrow, 5 anchors,
4 lobster claws,
an elephant's trunk,
a grandfather clock,
a fish hook, a fly,
3 keys, a lock,
a blue umbrella,
a black-billed gull,
a sword, a spyglass,
and a pirate skull!

Can you see
what I see?
2 boats in water,
10 birds in flight,
3 ice-cream cones,
a dragon kite,
a red flip-flop,
a crab, 2 maps,
a soccer ball,
3 bottle caps,
a pink flamingo,
a blue thumbtack,
and a parrot on
a postcard rack.

Can you see
what I see?
A bright red beak,
a whale's tail,
a white shark tooth,
a long jet trail,
2 loose buttons,
a blue airplane,
a dragonfly,
a weather vane,
3 wet seashells
in a stack –
It's time to pull
the towel back!

JOLLY ROGER

Can you see
what I see?
A frog, 5 starfish,
a bendy straw,
a fork, a feather,
a lobster claw,
a paper cup,
a ballpoint pen,
a washed-out tower,
a pirate's den,
a distant window
through an open door –
What's that treasure coin
that's washed ashore?

The Wreck of the BOUNTIFUL

Known Trade Routes

Known Pirate Routes

Possible Wreck Sites

Treasure Key

Black Rock

Bone Island